13/9/22

Dearest U. Eddie and A. Joyce

Enjoy see our lovely
country!

lots of love

Cheryl + Doug
(NZ)

NEW ZEALAND

UNTOUCHED LANDSCAPES

This book is dedicated with love to Kristina and Jakub for sharing this journey with me.

NEW ZEALAND
UNTOUCHED LANDSCAPES

PETR HLAVACEK

 potton & burton

PREFACE

I regard it as a great privilege to be able to work as a landscape photographer in New Zealand. The remarkable diversity of the landscapes on offer is quite astonishing, and it is hard to think of another place on our planet that could offer such an exhaustive range of extraordinary subject matter, so close at hand and compressed into such a small area. I have never lost the huge sense of gratitude I feel for being able to pursue my passion for photography in these wonderful islands.

My love of the natural world grew very organically, as I was raised in a tiny village in the middle of the Czech Republic, right on the edge of a large forest, and which was my playground as a child. Ironically, my love of the outdoors was strengthened when I had to serve my two years of, at that time, compulsory military service in an area of Šumava National Park, which is part of the Bohemian Forest. This area of forested highlands forms the border with my home country and Germany and Austria, and is as close to a genuine wilderness as you can get in Central Europe. It is here that my love for landscape photography really began.

As my interest in photography grew, I began to discover the work of Czech landscape photographers, in particular Karel Kuklík and Martin Milfort, who were producing beautiful images from this favourite part of my country. But I also started to open my eyes to wild landscapes in many other parts of the world through the flawless compositions of Ernst Haas, Ansel Adams, Clyde Butcher, and through the use of light and colour in the images of David Muench and Galen Rowell. All of these photographers provided huge inspiration, and the beginning of my understanding about composition, light and some of the technical aspects of taking a good landscape photograph.

But my journey as a photographer really started to become focussed when I moved to New Zealand and began work as a glacier guide on the Franz Josef Glacier. Here I became entranced by the spectacular shapes and colours of the ice-scapes I was seeing every day, and photographing these became a great obsession. From this, my photography has expanded, and while my heart remains very closely attached to the wilderness areas of South Westland, I have grown to love all of the untouched landscapes of New Zealand. This book is my tribute to these areas, my personal way of honouring their beauty and significance in this increasingly urbanised modern world.

— Petr Hlavacek

PREVIOUS PAGE: Sunset over Milford Sound, from Gertrude Saddle, Fiordland National Park

OVERLEAF: The Cook River, with Mt Tasman and Aoraki/Mt Cook beyond, from Gillespies Beach, Westland Tai Poutini National Park

ABOVE: Dawn at Scotts Beach, Heaphy Track, Kahurangi National Park
LEFT: Coastal forest on the Heaphy Track at Kohaihai, Kahurangi National Park
PREVIOUS PAGE: The Oparara River near Karamea, Kahurangi National Park

ABOVE: Morning light over Meybille Bay, north of Punakaiki, Paparoa National Park
LEFT: Coastline south of Charleston, West Coast
PREVIOUS PAGE: Sunset at the mouth of the Kohaihai River, Kahurangi National Park

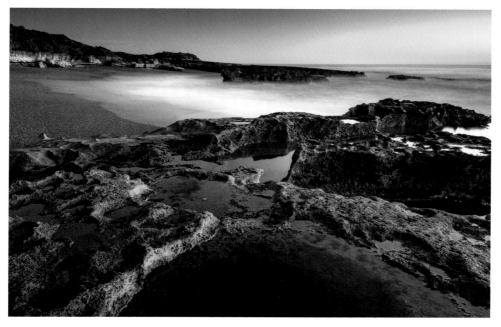

ABOVE: The beach at the base of Truman Track, Punakaiki, Paparoa National Park
LEFT: Coastal rocks near Rapahoe, West Coast

ABOVE: Sunset on the Pancake Rocks, Punakaiki, Paparoa National Park

LEFT: Looking south from Truman Track toward Punakaiki, Paparoa National Park

ABOVE: A waterfall on Bridal Veil Creek, Arthur's Pass National Park
LEFT: Ice Lake at the head of the Butler River, Westland
PREVIOUS PAGE: Twilight at the Pancake Rocks, Punakaiki,
Paparoa National Park

ABOVE: Forest edge, Lake Matheson,
Westland Tai Poutini National Park
LEFT: Sunrise at Lake Matheson, with Mt Tasman and
Aoraki/Mt Cook behind,
Westland Tai Poutini National Park
PREVIOUS PAGE: Hokitika Gorge, West Coast

ABOVE: A grove of kahikatea trees on farmland near Fox Glacier, with the Southern Alps beyond, South Westland
LEFT: Mt Tasman and Aoraki/Mt Cook from the beach at Three Mile Lagoon, Westland Tai Poutini National Park
OVERLEAF: Twilight at Gillespies Beach, with the moon rising over the head of the Fox Glacier, and Mt Tasman and Aoraki/Mt Cook to the right, Westland Tai Poutini National Park

ABOVE: Lake Mapourika with the Fritz Range behind,
Westland Tai Poutini National Park
LEFT: Winter mist, Lake Mapourika,
Westland Tai Poutini National Park
PREVIOUS PAGE: Kahikatea forest at sunrise,
Lake Wahapo, Westland Tai Poutini National Park

ABOVE: Ice formations on the Franz Josef Glacier, Westland Tai Poutini National Park
LEFT: The Franz Josef Glacier and southern rata in bloom, Westland Tai Poutini National Park
PREVIOUS PAGE: Wetland and kahikatea forest, Five Mile Lagoon, Westland Tai Poutini National Park

ABOVE: Crevasses at the head of the Fox Glacier, with
Mt Tasman behind, Westland Tai Poutini National Park
LEFT: Looking over the névé of the Fox Glacier, with
Mt Tasman and Aoraki/Mt Cook beyond,
Westland Tai Poutini National Park
PREVIOUS PAGE: Sunset on Three Mile Beach,
Westland Tai Poutini National Park

ABOVE: The Southern Alps, seen from Three Mile Beach near Okarito, Westland Tai Poutini National Park
PREVIOUS PAGE: Dawn at the Gillespies Lagoon, with the Fox Glacier beyond,
Westland Tai Poutini National Park

ABOVE: Sunset on the Southern Alps, seen from a coastal lagoon near Okarito, Westland Tai Poutini National Park
OVERLEAF: Coastal forest behind Three Mile Beach, with the Southern Alps at sunset,
Westland Tai Poutini National Park

ABOVE: Alpine plants near Castle Rock Hut,
Westland Tai Poutini National Park
LEFT: Franz Josef Glacier from Sentinel Rock,
Westland Tai Poutini National Park

ABOVE: Ice formations on the Franz Josef Glacier,
Westland Tai Poutini National Park
LEFT: Crevasses on the névé of the Fox Glacier, with Mt Tasman
to the right, Westland Tai Poutini National Park
PREVIOUS PAGE: The vista from Mt Fox, with the Fox Glacier
on the left, and Mt Tasman and Aoraki/Mt Cook centre,
Westland Tai Poutini National Park

ABOVE: Sunset on the beach at Ship Creek near Haast, South Westland
LEFT: Forest near Lake Mahinapua, Westland
PREVIOUS PAGE: Alpine vistas with Fox Glacier and the Southern Alps in cloud,
Westland Tai Poutini National Park

ABOVE: A side-creek in the Butler Valley, Westland
LEFT: The Copland River, Westland Tai Poutini National Park
PREVIOUS PAGE: The Smoothwater River, near Jackson Bay
OVERLEAF: The Arawhata River near Jackson Bay,
South Westland

ABOVE AND LEFT: Tarns on Key Summit, Fiordland National Park
PREVIOUS PAGE: The Thunder Falls and Haast River near Haast Pass, South Westland

ABOVE: Bowen Falls in Milford Sound, Fiordland National Park
LEFT: Looking down on the Routeburn Flats from the
Routeburn Track, Mount Aspiring National Park
PREVIOUS PAGE: Beech forest near Lake Mackenzie on the
Routeburn Track, Fiordland National Park

ABOVE: Looking down on Lake Mackenzie, Routeburn Track, Fiordland National Park
PREVIOUS PAGE: Lake Mackenzie, Routeburn Track, Fiordland National Park

ABOVE: Lake Harris and Conical Hill, Routeburn Track, Mount Aspiring National Park
OVERLEAF: Sub-alpine forest near Greenstone Saddle, with the Livingstone Mountains beyond, Fiordland National Park

ABOVE: Bowen Falls, Milford Sound, Fiordland National Park
LEFT: Milford Sound with Mitre Peak, Fiordland National Park
PREVIOUS PAGE: Mitre Peak and Milford Sound on a winter morning, Fiordland National Park
OVERLEAF: Dramatic winter sunset, Milford Sound, Fiordland National Park

ABOVE: Above the West Matukituki Valley, Mount Aspiring National Park
LEFT: The West Matukituki River with Mt Aspiring/Tititea beyond.
PREVIOUS PAGE: Sunrise over the Hope Arm of Lake Manapouri,
with The Monument on the left, Fiordland National Park

ABOVE: Icebergs in the Hooker Lake, Hooker Valley,
Aoraki/Mount Cook National Park
LEFT: Icebergs in the Hooker Lake with Aoraki/Mt Cook
behind, Aoraki/Mount Cook National Park
PREVIOUS PAGE: Sunrise over Lake Wanaka,
seen from Roys Peak, Central Otago

ABOVE: Sunset on Aoraki/Mt Cook,
Aoraki/Mount Cook National Park
LEFT: Winter morning in the Hooker Valley, with Aoraki/
Mt Cook behind, Aoraki/Mount Cook National Park

ABOVE: The outlet of the Mueller Lake with Mt Sefton and
The Footstool beyond, Aoraki/Mount Cook National Park
LEFT: The eastern faces of Mt Sefton and The Footstool,
with the terminal lake of the Mueller Glacier
OVERLEAF: The terminal face and lake of the Tasman Glacier,
with the glacier beyond, Aoraki/Mount Cook National Park

LEFT: Lake Pukaki with Aoraki/Mt Cook above the head of the lake
PREVIOUS PAGE: Dawn over the Tasman Glacier from Ball Ridge, with De la Beche beyond, Aoraki/Mount Cook National Park

ABOVE: Petrified tree trunks at
Curio Bay, The Catlins
LEFT: Sunrise at Nugget Point, The Catlins
PREVIOUS PAGE: Lake Tekapo and the
Southern Alps, Mackenzie Country

ABOVE: Tahakopa Bay near Papatowai, The Catlins
LEFT: Dawn at Nugget Point, The Catlins
PREVIOUS PAGE: Sunset over the coastline south of Nugget Point, The Catlins

ABOVE: Dusk over Hinapouri Tarn, with the St Arnaud Range beyond, Nelson Lakes National Park
LEFT: Looking north over Hinapouri Tarn and Lake Angelus to Tasman Bay in the distance
PREVIOUS PAGE: Looking up the Waimakariri River to the Southern Alps, Arthur's Pass National Park
OVERLEAF: Sunset over Lake Rotoroa, Nelson Lakes National Park

ABOVE: Sunset at Marahau, looking toward Abel Tasman National Park
LEFT: Evening over the Archway Islands, Wharariki Beach,
west coast of Golden Bay
PREVIOUS PAGE: Sunrise from Mt Stokes, outer Marlborough Sounds

ABOVE AND LEFT: Sunset over Whanganui Inlet,
west coast of Golden Bay
PREVIOUS PAGE: Coastal rock formations, Totaranui,
Abel Tasman National Park

ABOVE: Coastal rock formations at Paturau, west coast of Golden Bay
LEFT: Sunset over the coastline south of Paturau, west coast of Golden Bay
OVERLEAF: Sunrise over Farewell Spit, Golden Bay

LEFT: First light on volcanic landscape under Mt Ruapehu, Tongariro National Park
PREVIOUS PAGE: Blue Lake and Mt Ngauruhoe, Tongariro National Park

ABOVE: Sunset over Mt Ngauruhoe,
Tongariro National Park
LEFT: Sunrise over Blue Lake and
Mt Ngauruhoe, Tongariro National Park
OVERLEAF: The Rangipo Desert and
Mt Ruapehu, Tongariro National Park

ABOVE: Mountain cabbage trees,
Egmont National Park
LEFT: Sunset over Mt Taranaki, from the
Pouakai Range, Egmont National Park
PREVIOUS PAGE: Morning light on
Mt Taranaki, from the Pouakai Range,
Egmont National Park

ABOVE: Cape Egmont lighthouse, Taranaki
LEFT: Remains of the Three Sisters,
Taranaki coastline

ABOVE AND LEFT: Mist swirling through beech trees, Panekiri Range, Te Urewera
PREVIOUS PAGE: Sunrise over Lake Waikaremoana, Te Urewera

ABOVE AND LEFT: Korokoro Falls, Lake Waikaremoana, Te Urewera
PREVIOUS PAGE: Korokoro Stream, Lake Waikaremoana, Te Urewera
OVERLEAF: Sunset over Lake Waikaremoana, Te Urewera

First published in 2016 by Potton & Burton

Potton & Burton
98 Vickerman Street, PO Box 5128, Nelson, New Zealand
www.pottonandburton.co.nz

Photography © Petr Hlavacek

ISBN 978 0 947503 20 8

Printed in China by Midas Printing International Ltd